ISBN: 978-1-969801-00-6
© 2025
Printed in the USA

Introduction

Welcome to *Winning the War Within*, a Bible study focused on the timeless struggle every believer faces—resisting temptation and staying faithful to God.

Throughout history, Christians have wrestled with subtle distractions, doubts, and temptations that threaten to weaken faith. This book is designed to help you recognize those struggles for what they are: spiritual battles. By turning to Scripture, prayer, and reflection, you can learn to stand firm and walk more closely with Christ.

While the themes in this study are inspired in part by C.S. Lewis's *The Screwtape Letters*, this book is not a summary or retelling of his work. Instead, it is a Scripture-based guide that draws lessons from the same spiritual truths, helping today's Christian grow stronger in faith.

Who Is This Study Guide For?

This study is written for anyone who desires to grow stronger in their walk with Christ. It is suitable for individuals seeking a personal journey of faith, for small groups who want to engage in meaningful conversations about spiritual warfare, and for church leaders or teachers in need of a structured resource that provides both depth and practical application. Whether you are new to Christianity or have been following Christ for many years, *Winning the War Within* offers encouragement and guidance to help you recognize temptation, resist distractions, and remain firmly rooted in God's Word.

How To Use This Study Guide

Each session in this book highlights a key theme of spiritual warfare, supported by Scripture passages, reflection questions, and real-world applications.

To get the most out of this study:

1. **Begin with prayer** — Ask God to guide your heart and mind as you learn.
2. **Read the session theme** — Each chapter introduces a specific area of spiritual struggle and growth.
3. **Reflect on Scripture** — Passages are included to help anchor your thoughts in God's Word.
4. **Engage with the questions** — Use them for personal reflection or group discussion.
5. **Apply what you learn** — Each session ends with practical ways to live out the truths you've studied.

This study can be completed individually, with a partner, or in a small group setting. It is flexible enough to be used in weekly gatherings, church classes, or personal devotional time.

"Your word is a lamp to my feet and a light to my path."
— Psalm 119:105

The Quiet Road to Ruin

Readers working through this study alongside
The Screwtape Letters may wish to revisit Chapter 1

Chapter 1 Major Takeaways

In Chapter One we are introduced to Screwtape, a senior demon, who is writing letters to his nephew, Wormwood, a junior tempter. Screwtape offers advice on how to lead a human (referred to as "the Patient") away from God ("the Enemy"). He criticizes Wormwood for being too focused on tempting the Patient with grand sins. Instead, Screwtape advises using small, subtle distractions to keep the Patient away from spiritual thoughts and actions. He emphasizes the importance of keeping the Patient preoccupied with the ordinary and mundane aspects of life to prevent any consideration of spiritual matters or the existence of God.

Discussion Questions

1. What strategies does Screwtape suggest Wormwood use to distract the Patient from spiritual matters?

"Be of sober spirit, be watchful. Your adversary, the devil, prowls around like a roaring lion, seeking someone to devour."
1 Peter 5:8

2. How does Screwtape's advice reflect on the nature of temptation in our everyday lives?

"Put on the full armor of God, so that you will be able to stand firm against the schemes of the devil. For our struggle is not against flesh and blood, but against the rulers, against the authorities, against the world forces of this darkness, against the spiritual forces of wickedness in heavenly the places. Therefore, take up the full armor of God, so that you will be able to resist in the evil day, and having done everything, to stand firm."
Ephesians 6:11-13

3. Why does Screwtape prefer small, seemingly insignificant distractions over major sins?

"Be subject therefore to God. Resist the devil and he will flee from you."
James 4:7

4. How can we guard ourselves against the "small distractions" that Screwtape recommends?

"But seek first His kingdom and His righteousness, and all these things will be added to you."
Matthew 6:33

5. What role does busyness play in our spiritual lives, according to Screwtape? How can we counteract this?

"Finally, brothers, whatever is true, whatever is dignified, whatever is right, whatever is pure, whatever is lovely, whatever is commendable, if there is any excellence and if anything worthy of praise, consider these things."
Philippians 4:8

6. What is the significance of Screwtape's focus on the Patient's perceptions and feelings rather than objective reality?

"There is a way which seems right to a man, but its end is the way of death."
Proverbs 14:12

REAL WORLD APPLICATIONS

PRACTICE MINDFULNESS AND INTENTIONAL LIVING. BE AWARE OF HOW YOU SPEND YOUR TIME AND WHERE YOUR ATTENTION GOES THROUGHOUT THE DAY. SIMPLE ACTIVITIES LIKE SETTING ASIDE SPECIFIC TIMES FOR PRAYER, MEDITATION, OR BIBLE STUDY CAN HELP MAINTAIN SPIRITUAL FOCUS.

2

The Fellowship Barrier

Readers working through this study alongside
The Screwtape Letters may wish to revisit Chapter 2

Chapter 2 Major Takeaways

In Chapter Two, Screwtape responds to Wormwood's dismay over the Patient's recent conversion to Christianity. Screwtape reassures Wormwood that all is not lost and provides strategies to undermine the Patient's newfound faith. He suggests leveraging the Patient's disappointment with the church, particularly the behavior of fellow churchgoers, to foster feelings of disillusionment and hypocrisy. Screwtape advises focusing on the flaws and annoyances within the church community to create a sense of self-righteousness and disdain in the Patient.

Discussion Questions

1. How does Screwtape suggest Wormwood exploit the Patient's experience in church to weaken his faith?

"And let us consider how to stimulate one another to love and good deeds, not forsaking our own assembling together, as is the habit of some, but encouraging one another, and all the more as you see the day drawing near."
Hebrews 10:24-25

2. What are the potential dangers of focusing on the flaws of fellow believers, according to Screwtape?

"Therefore let us not judge one another anymore, but rather judge this—not to put a stumbling block or offense before a brother."
Romans 14:13

3. Why does Screwtape believe the Patient's expectations of the church can be a tool for temptation?

"bearing with one another, and graciously forgiving each other, whoever has a complaint against anyone, just as the Lord graciously forgave you, so also should you."
Colossians 3:13

4. How can we counteract the feelings of disillusionment that Screwtape advises Wormwood to foster?

"with all humility and gentleness, with patience, bearing with one another in love, [3] being diligent to keep the unity of the Spirit in the bond of peace."
Ephesians 4:2-3

5. What does Screwtape mean by "the Patient's ideas of 'the real' Church"? How can this concept be both helpful and harmful?

"Do not judge, so that you will not be judged. For with what judgment you judge, you will be judged; and with what measure you measure, it will be measured to you."
Matthew 7:1-2

6. How can focusing on one's own spiritual growth help mitigate the temptation to judge others in the church?

"Test yourselves to see if you are in the faith; examine yourselves! Or do you not recognize about yourselves that Jesus Christ is in you— unless indeed you fail the test?"
2 Corinthians 13:5

REAL WORLD APPLICATIONS

WHEN ATTENDING CHURCH OR ENGAGING WITH A FAITH COMMUNITY, FOCUS ON THE POSITIVE ASPECTS AND CONTRIBUTIONS OF FELLOW MEMBERS RATHER THAN THEIR FAULTS OR IMPERFECTIONS. THIS SHIFT IN PERSPECTIVE FOSTERS UNITY AND ENCOURAGEMENT, HELPING TO STRENGTHEN PERSONAL FAITH AND COMMUNITY BONDS DESPITE HUMAN FLAWS.

3 🪶

Home Front Hostilities

*Readers working through this study alongside
The Screwtape Letters may wish to revisit Chapter 3*

Chapter 3 Major Takeaways

In Chapter Three, Screwtape focuses on the Patient's relationship with his mother. Screwtape advises Wormwood to exploit the daily annoyances and frustrations the Patient feels towards her to foster anger and resentment. He suggests encouraging the Patient to pray for his mother's "spiritual needs" in a way that focuses on her faults rather than genuinely seeking her well-being. Screwtape also advises making both the Patient and his mother hypersensitive to each other's irritations and faults, further straining their relationship and distracting the Patient from his spiritual growth.

Discussion Questions

1. What tactics does Screwtape suggest to strain the Patient's relationship with his mother?

"Let all bitterness and anger and wrath and shouting and slander be put away from you, along with all malice. Instead, be kind to one another, tender-hearted, graciously forgiving each other, just as God in Christ also has graciously forgiven you."
Ephesians 4:31-32

2. How does Screwtape advise Wormwood to twist the Patient's prayers for his mother?

"bearing with one another, and graciously forgiving each other, whoever has a complaint against anyone, just as the Lord graciously forgave you, so also should you."
Colossians 3:13

3. What role does hypersensitivity play in the strategies suggested by Screwtape?

"Know this, my beloved brothers. But everyone must be quick to hear, slow to speak and slow to anger; for the anger of man does not achieve the righteousness of God."
James 1:19-20

4. How can the Patient's experience with his mother illustrate the broader theme of relationships in spiritual warfare?

"doing nothing¹from selfish ambition or vain glory, but with humility of mind regarding one another as more important than yourselves, not merely looking out for your own personal interests, but also for the interests of others."
Philippians 2:3-4

5. What practical steps can we take to prevent resentment and anger from taking root in our relationships?

"But I say to you, love your enemies and pray for those who persecute you,"
Matthew 5:44

6. Why does Screwtape emphasize focusing on "unseen" irritations and how can we counteract this in our own lives?

"But Yahweh said to Samuel, 'Do not look at his appearance or at the height of his stature, because I have rejected him; for God sees not as man sees, for man looks at the outward appearance, but Yahweh looks at the heart.'"
1 Samuel 16:7

REAL WORLD APPLICATIONS

IN YOUR RELATIONSHIPS, ESPECIALLY WITH FAMILY MEMBERS, CHOOSE TO EMPHASIZE UNDERSTANDING, PATIENCE, AND FORGIVENESS OVER FOCUSING ON THEIR FLAWS AND ANNOYANCES. THIS APPROACH NURTURES HEALTHIER, MORE SUPPORTIVE RELATIONSHIPS AND PREVENTS MINOR IRRITATIONS FROM GROWING INTO SIGNIFICANT CONFLICTS, THEREBY STRENGTHENING BOTH YOUR PERSONAL BONDS AND SPIRITUAL WELL-BEING.

4

Prayer Without Connection

Readers working through this study alongside
The Screwtape Letters may wish to revisit Chapter 4

Chapter 4 Major Takeaways

In Chapter Four, Screwtape discusses the subject of prayer. He advises Wormwood to prevent the Patient from developing a sincere prayer life. Screwtape suggests encouraging the Patient to focus on his feelings during prayer rather than the act of praying itself. He also recommends promoting a vague and abstract idea of God, making the Patient's prayers less effective. By keeping the Patient's prayers superficial and self-centered, Wormwood can hinder the Patient's spiritual growth and relationship with God.

Discussion Questions

1. What strategies does Screwtape suggest Wormwood use to weaken the Patient's prayer life?

"And when you are praying, do not use meaningless repetition as the Gentiles do, for they suppose that they will be heard for their many words."
Matthew 6:7

2. How does focusing on feelings during prayer, as Screwtape suggests, detract from the true purpose of prayer?

"Be anxious for nothing, but in everything by prayer and petition with thanksgiving let your requests be made known to God."
Philippians 4:6

3. Why does Screwtape want the Patient to have a vague and abstract idea of God?

"Therefore, confess your sins to one another, and pray for one another so that you may be healed. The effective prayer of a righteous man can accomplish much."
James 5:16

4. How can we ensure that our prayers are sincere and focused on God rather than on our own emotions or expectations?

"And in the same way the Spirit also helps our weakness, for we do not know how to pray as we should, but the Spirit Himself intercedes for us with groanings too deep for words;"
Romans 8:26

5. What impact does Screwtape believe superficial and self-centered prayers will have on the Patient's spiritual life?

"Pray, then, in this way: 'Our Father who is in heaven, Hallowed be Your name. Your kingdom come. Your will be done, On earth as it is in heaven. Give us this day our daily bread. And forgive us our debts, as we also have forgiven our debtors. And do not lead us into temptation, but deliver us from the evil one. For Yours is the kingdom and the power and the glory forever. Amen.'"
Matthew 6:9-13

6. How can we guard against the distractions and misconceptions about prayer that Screwtape recommends?

"Devote yourselves to prayer, being watchful in it with thanksgiving;"
Colossians 4:2

REAL WORLD APPLICATIONS

WHEN PRAYING, AVOID FOCUSING ON HOW YOU FEEL IN THE MOMENT. INSTEAD, PRIORITIZE CONSISTENCY AND GENUINE CONNECTION WITH GOD. BY NOT RELYING ON EMOTIONS, YOU'LL CULTIVATE A MORE STABLE AND ENDURING PRAYER LIFE, HELPING YOU STAY SPIRITUALLY GROUNDED EVEN DURING TIMES WHEN YOU MAY NOT "FEEL" CLOSE TO GOD. THIS APPROACH STRENGTHENS YOUR FAITH THROUGH DISCIPLINE AND COMMITMENT.

Profiting From Panic

*Readers working through this study alongside
The Screwtape Letters may wish to revisit Chapter 5*

Chapter 5 Major Takeaways

In Chapter Five, Screwtape discusses the outbreak of war (likely referencing World War II) and its effects on the Patient. Wormwood is excited about the potential for destruction and fear, but Screwtape advises caution. He explains that while war can produce immediate fear and suffering, it also has the potential to drive people closer to God, especially when faced with their mortality. Screwtape warns that war can evoke virtues like courage and self-sacrifice, which are dangerous to their cause. He encourages Wormwood to exploit the fear and anxiety associated with war but to be wary of its potential to turn people towards faith and repentance.

Discussion Questions

1. Why does Screwtape caution Wormwood about the effects of war on the Patient's faith?

"When I am afraid, I will trust in You."
Psalm 56:3

2. How can fear and anxiety during times of crisis be both a tool for temptation and an opportunity for spiritual growth?

"And we know that for those who love God [a]all things work together for good, for those who are called according to His purpose."
Romans 8:28

3. What virtues does Screwtape fear might be awakened in the Patient during the war? Why are these dangerous to their cause?

"For God has not given us a spirit of [a]timidity, but of power and love and [b]self-discipline."
2 Timothy 1:7

4. How might the Patient's awareness of his own mortality influence his spiritual life, according to Screwtape?

"These things I have spoken to you, so that in Me you may have peace. In the world you have tribulation, but take courage; I have overcome the world.""
John 16:33

5. In what ways can we seek to cultivate virtues like courage and self-sacrifice during times of fear or crisis?

"Consider it all joy, my brothers, when you encounter various trials, knowing that the testing of your faith brings about perseverance. And let perseverance have its perfect work, so that you may be perfect and complete, lacking in nothing."
James 1:2-4

6. What strategies can we use to turn fear and anxiety into opportunities for strengthening our faith?

"Have I not commanded you? Be strong and courageous! Do not be in dread or be dismayed, for Yahweh your God is with you wherever you go."
Joshua 1:9

REAL WORLD APPLICATIONS

RESIST THE TEMPTATION TO BECOME COMPLACENT DURING PEACEFUL TIMES. INSTEAD, USE THESE MOMENTS TO STRENGTHEN YOUR SPIRITUAL LIFE BY STAYING DISCIPLINED IN PRAYER, SCRIPTURE READING, AND COMMUNITY INVOLVEMENT. BY DOING SO, YOU BUILD A STRONG FOUNDATION THAT WILL HELP YOU REMAIN STEADFAST IN YOUR FAITH WHEN CHALLENGES OR TRIALS ARISE.

6

The Tyranny of 'What If'

Readers working through this study alongside
The Screwtape Letters may wish to revisit Chapter 6

Chapter 6 Major Takeaways

In Chapter Six, Screwtape advises Wormwood to exploit the Patient's fears and anxieties about the future, particularly in the context of the ongoing war. He suggests keeping the Patient focused on potential future troubles and uncertainties, rather than on the present or on his relationship with God. Screwtape also encourages Wormwood to foster feelings of hatred toward the Patient's enemies while making sure that the Patient believes he is being righteous in his hatred. Screwtape emphasizes the importance of keeping the Patient's mind divided between his fear of the future and his hatred of others, thereby preventing him from focusing on spiritual growth and trust in God.

Discussion Questions

1. How does Screwtape suggest Wormwood use the Patient's fears about the future to distract him from spiritual growth?

"So do not worry about tomorrow; for tomorrow will worry about itself. [a]Each day has enough trouble of its own."
Matthew 6:34

2. Why does Screwtape emphasize the importance of keeping the Patient's mind focused on the future rather than the present?

"Be anxious for nothing, but in everything by prayer and petition with thanksgiving let your requests be made known to God. [7] And the peace of God, which surpasses all [a]comprehension, will guard your hearts and your minds in Christ Jesus."
Philippians 4:6-7

3. How does Screwtape propose using the Patient's hatred toward his enemies to weaken his faith?

"The one who says he is in the Light and yet hates his brother is in the darkness until now."
1 John 2:9

4. What does Screwtape mean by dividing the Patient's mind, and how can this division be detrimental to his spiritual life?

"But I say to you, love your enemies and pray for those who persecute you,"
Matthew 5:44

5. How can we counteract the temptation to be consumed by fear of the future or hatred toward others?

"Trust in Yahweh with all your heart And do not lean on your own understanding. In all your ways acknowledge Him, And He will make your paths straight."
Proverbs 3:5-6

6. What role does trust in God's plan play in overcoming the fears and anxieties discussed by Screwtape?

"When I am afraid, I will trust in You. In God, whose word I praise, In God I trust; I shall not be afraid. What can mere man do to me?"
Psalm 56:3–4

REAL WORLD APPLICATIONS

BE MINDFUL OF HOW SMALL IRRITATIONS CAN GROW INTO LARGER RESENTMENTS. WHEN YOU FEEL ANNOYED BY SOMEONE, PRACTICE FORGIVENESS AND EMPATHY IMMEDIATELY, FOCUSING ON THE POSITIVE ASPECTS OF THE RELATIONSHIP. THIS HELPS PREVENT MINOR ISSUES FROM ESCALATING INTO BIGGER CONFLICTS, FOSTERING HEALTHIER AND MORE LOVING RELATIONSHIPS IN YOUR DAILY LIFE.

7

The Politics of Division

Readers working through this study alongside
The Screwtape Letters may wish to revisit Chapter 7

Chapter 7 Major Takeaways

In Chapter Seven, Screwtape advises Wormwood on how to manipulate the Patient's beliefs about the existence of devils. He suggests two approaches: either to make the Patient skeptical of their existence, dismissing them as myth, or to make him an extreme believer, obsessed with demons and the occult. Screwtape emphasizes that either extreme—disbelief or obsession—can be equally useful in undermining the Patient's spiritual life. Screwtape also discusses how to exploit the Patient's political views, encouraging him to focus more on political causes than on his faith, and to make his politics an integral part of his religion. This can lead to division, self-righteousness, and a diluted focus on God.

Discussion Questions

1. Why does Screwtape suggest that either disbelief in devils or an obsession with them can be useful in undermining the Patient's faith?

"When I am afraid, I will trust in You. In God, whose word I praise, In God I trust; I shall not be afraid. What can mere man do to me?"
Psalm 56:3–4

2. How does Screwtape propose to use the Patient's political views to weaken his faith?

"Be of sober spirit, be watchful. Your adversary the devil prowls around like a roaring lion, seeking someone to devour."
1 Peter 5:8

3. What are the potential dangers of integrating politics too deeply with one's faith, according to Screwtape?

"Then He said to them, 'Therefore render to Caesar the things that are Caesar's; and to God the things that are God's.'"
Matthew 22:21

4. How can a balanced understanding of spiritual forces help maintain a healthy and grounded faith?

"For our citizenship is in heaven, from which also we eagerly wait for a Savior, the Lord Jesus Christ."
Philippians 3:20

5. What practical steps can we take to ensure that our political beliefs do not overshadow our primary focus on God?

"But refuse foolish and ignorant speculations, knowing that they produce quarrels. And the Lord's slave must not be quarrelsome, but be kind to all, able to teach, patient when wronged."
2 Timothy 2:23-24

6. How can we guard against the extremes of either denying or obsessing over spiritual forces like devils and demons?

"So that no advantage would be taken of us by Satan, for we are not ignorant of his schemes."
2 Corinthians 2:11

REAL WORLD APPLICATIONS

AVOID LETTING YOUR BELIEFS BECOME A SOURCE OF DIVISION OR SUPERIORITY OVER OTHERS. INSTEAD, FOCUS ON LIVING OUT YOUR FAITH WITH HUMILITY AND LOVE, RESPECTING DIFFERENT PERSPECTIVES. BY DOING SO, YOU CAN AVOID PRIDE AND MAINTAIN UNITY AND COMPASSION IN YOUR RELATIONSHIPS, ENSURING THAT YOUR FAITH IS A BRIDGE RATHER THAN A BARRIER.

8

The Law of Undulation

Readers working through this study alongside
The Screwtape Letters may wish to revisit Chapter 8

Chapter 8 Major Takeaways

In Chapter Eight, Screwtape introduces the concept of "the law of Undulation," which he describes as the natural rhythm of life that includes periods of highs (spiritual and emotional peaks) and lows (spiritual and emotional troughs). Screwtape explains that all humans experience these fluctuations in their spiritual lives. He warns Wormwood that during the Patient's low points, God may be working to build a more mature, resilient faith in the Patient, even if he feels distant from God during these times. Screwtape advises that during these trough periods, Wormwood should tempt the Patient with feelings of despair, doubt, and the belief that his faith was merely a passing phase. However, he also cautions that if the Patient learns to trust God even in the troughs, his faith may actually grow stronger.

Discussion Questions

1. What is "the law of Undulation" as described by Screwtape, and how does it affect the Patient's spiritual life?

"Consider it all joy, my brothers, when you encounter various trials,
knowing that the testing of your faith brings about perseverance.
And let perseverance have its perfect work, so that you may be
perfect and complete, lacking in nothing."
James 1:2-4

2. Why does Screwtape warn that the trough periods can be dangerous for their cause?

"Even though I walk through the valley of the shadow of death, I fear no evil, for You are with me; Your rod and Your staff, they comfort me."
Psalm 23:4

3. How can understanding the law of Undulation help us in our own spiritual journeys?

"And He has said to me, 'My grace is sufficient for you, for power is perfected in weakness.' Most gladly, therefore, I will rather boast in my weaknesses, so that the power of Christ may dwell in me. Therefore I am well content with weaknesses, with insults, with distresses, with persecutions, with hardships, for the sake of Christ; for when I am weak, then I am strong."
2 Corinthians 12:9-10

4. Why might God allow us to experience spiritual lows, according to Screwtape's insights?

"And we know that for those who love God all things work together for good, for those who are called according to His purpose."
Romans 8:28

5. What strategies can we use to remain faithful during the spiritual low points described in this chapter?

"Now faith is the assurance of things hoped for, the conviction of things not seen."
Hebrews 11:1

6. How can the awareness of spiritual peaks and troughs influence our expectations of the Christian life?

"For momentary, light affliction is producing for us an eternal weight of glory far beyond all comparison, while we look not at the things which are seen, but at the things which are not seen; for the things which are seen are temporal, but the things which are not seen are eternal."
2 Corinthians 4:17–18

REAL WORLD APPLICATIONS

UNDERSTAND THAT SPIRITUAL LIFE HAS UPS AND DOWNS. DURING LOW POINTS, REMAIN FAITHFUL AND CONTINUE YOUR SPIRITUAL PRACTICES, TRUSTING THAT GOD IS STILL AT WORK. BY STAYING COMMITTED DURING THESE DRY PERIODS, YOU BUILD A DEEPER, MORE RESILIENT FAITH THAT CAN WITHSTAND CHALLENGES AND GROW STRONGER OVER TIME.

9 🪶

Pleasure Twisted, Purpose Lost

Readers working through this study alongside
The Screwtape Letters may wish to revisit Chapter 9

Chapter 9 Major Takeaways

In Chapter Nine, Screwtape advises Wormwood on how to take advantage of the Patient's trough period, where his spiritual life is in a low phase. Screwtape suggests tempting the Patient with sensual pleasures, such as sexual temptation or indulgence in food and drink, as these are more effective during times of spiritual dryness. Screwtape also recommends encouraging the Patient to look for a "feeling" of spirituality, leading him to mistake emotional experiences for true faith. If Wormwood can make the Patient seek after spiritual highs rather than a genuine relationship with God, the Patient may become more focused on his own emotions rather than on God Himself.

Discussion Questions

1. Why does Screwtape believe that sensual temptations are more effective during the Patient's trough periods?

"Be of sober spirit, be watchful. Your adversary the devil prowls around like a roaring lion, seeking someone to devour. But resist him, firm in the faith, knowing that the same experiences of suffering are

being accomplished among your brethren who are in the world."
1 Peter 5:8-9

2. How does Screwtape suggest Wormwood can use the Patient's desire for spiritual feelings to his advantage?

"But each one is tempted when he is carried away and enticed by his own lust. Then when lust has conceived, it gives birth to sin, and when sin is fully matured, it brings forth death."
James 1:14-15

3. What dangers does Screwtape highlight about the Patient confusing emotional highs with true spiritual growth?

"But I say, walk by the Spirit and you will not carry out the desire of the flesh."
Galatians 5:16

4. How can the pursuit of pleasure during spiritual lows be a distraction from true spiritual growth?

"For we walk by faith, not by sight."
2 Corinthians 5:7

5. What practical steps can we take to resist the temptations that come during our spiritual troughs?

> *"Create in me a clean heart, O God, And renew a steadfast spirit within me."*
> *Psalm 51:10*

6. How can we cultivate a faith that is not dependent on feelings but on a steady relationship with God?

> *"For the righteous man falls seven times and rises again, But the wicked stumble in time of calamity."*
> *Proverbs 24:16*

REAL WORLD APPLICATIONS

WHEN YOU EXPERIENCE SPIRITUAL LOWS, AVOID SEEKING QUICK FIXES OR DISTRACTIONS. INSTEAD, USE THESE TIMES TO DEEPEN YOUR FAITH BY CONTINUING YOUR SPIRITUAL PRACTICES AND REFLECTING ON GOD'S PRESENCE IN ALL CIRCUMSTANCES. THIS APPROACH HELPS YOU GROW STRONGER SPIRITUALLY, TURNING CHALLENGES INTO OPPORTUNITIES FOR GROWTH RATHER THAN ALLOWING THEM TO LEAD YOU ASTRAY.

10

Friends In Low Places

Readers working through this study alongside
The Screwtape Letters may wish to revisit Chapter 10

Chapter 10 Major Takeaways

In Chapter Ten, Screwtape rejoices that the Patient has made new friends who are wealthy, worldly, and not Christians. Screwtape sees this as an opportunity to draw the Patient away from his faith by encouraging him to adopt the values and behaviors of his new social circle. Screwtape advises Wormwood to use the Patient's desire to fit in and be accepted by his friends to gradually erode his spiritual convictions. By making the Patient lead a double life—one where he pretends to hold the same values as his friends while still trying to maintain his Christian beliefs—Screwtape hopes to create internal conflict and eventually weaken the Patient's faith.

Discussion Questions

1. How does Screwtape plan to use the Patient's new friendships to lead him away from his faith?

"Do not be deceived: 'Bad company corrupts good morals.'"
1 Corinthians 15:33

2. What are the risks of the Patient leading a double life, as Screwtape suggests?

"You adulteresses, do you not know that friendship with the world is hostility toward God? Therefore whoever wishes to be a friend of the world sets himself as an enemy of God."
James 4:4

3. Why might the desire to fit in with worldly friends be particularly tempting for the Patient?

"He who walks with wise men will be wise, But a companion of fools will suffer harm."
Proverbs 13:20

4. How can we recognize when our relationships are leading us away from our faith rather than supporting it?

"You are the light of the world. A city set on a hill cannot be hidden; nor does anyone light a lamp and put it under a basket, but on the lampstand, and it gives light to all who are in the house. Let your light shine before men in such a way that they may see your good works, and glorify your Father who is in heaven."
Matthew 5:14-16

5. What strategies can we use to maintain our faith and values even when surrounded by non-Christian influences?

"And do not be conformed to this world, but be transformed by the renewing of your mind, so that you may approve what the will of God is, that which is good and pleasing and perfect."
Romans 12:2

6. How can living a consistent, authentic Christian life impact both ourselves and those around us?

"Better is a poor man who walks in his integrity Than one who is crooked in speech and is a fool."
Proverbs 19:1

REAL WORLD APPLICATIONS

BE CAUTIOUS ABOUT THE INFLUENCE OF NEW FRIENDSHIPS OR SOCIAL CIRCLES THAT MAY LEAD YOU AWAY FROM YOUR VALUES. STAY GROUNDED IN YOUR FAITH AND BELIEFS, EVEN WHEN INTEGRATING INTO NEW GROUPS. BY MAINTAINING YOUR SPIRITUAL INTEGRITY, YOU CAN POSITIVELY INFLUENCE OTHERS RATHER THAN BEING SWAYED INTO COMPROMISING YOUR PRINCIPLES.

11

Laughter Without Light

Readers working through this study alongside
The Screwtape Letters may wish to revisit Chapter 11

Chapter 11 Major Takeaways

In Chapter Eleven, Screwtape discusses the different types of laughter and how each can be used to the demons' advantage. He distinguishes between four kinds of laughter: Joy, Fun, the Joke Proper, and Flippancy. Joy, according to Screwtape, is of little use to the devils because it tends to elevate people and connect them with others in a wholesome way. Fun, which is related to Joy but less profound, can also be harmless unless it distracts from more serious matters. The Joke Proper can be useful, particularly when it involves making light of serious matters, leading to a gradual erosion of respect for important truths. Flippancy, however, is the most effective tool for the devils, as it leads to a dismissive attitude toward everything, fostering cynicism and making it difficult for the Patient to take anything, including his faith, seriously.

Discussion Questions

1. How does Screwtape categorize the different types of laughter, and why is Flippancy considered the most dangerous?

"A joyful heart is good medicine, But a broken spirit dries up the
bones."
Proverbs 17:22

2. Why does Screwtape see little value in Joy and Fun as tools for temptation?

> "A time to weep and a time to laugh; A time to mourn and a time to dance."
> Ecclesiastes 3:4

3. How can the "Joke Proper" be used to undermine respect for important values and truths?

> "And there must be no filthiness and silly talk, or coarse jesting, which are not fitting, but rather giving of thanks."
> Ephesians 5:4

4. What are the potential spiritual dangers of adopting a flippant attitude toward life and faith?

> "Rejoice in the Lord always; again I will say, rejoice!"
> Philippians 4:4

5. How can we cultivate a healthy sense of humor that does not compromise our spiritual values?

"But now you also, lay them all aside: wrath, anger, malice, slander, and abusive speech from your mouth."
Colossians 3:8

6. In what ways can Joy and Fun be incorporated into a Christian life to enhance spiritual health?

"The heart of the discerning seeks knowledge, But the mouth of fools feeds on folly."
Proverbs 15:14

REAL WORLD APPLICATIONS

BE MINDFUL OF HOW HUMOR IS USED IN YOUR LIFE. WHILE LAUGHTER IS VALUABLE, AVOID SARCASM OR FLIPPANCY THAT BELITTLES IMPORTANT VALUES OR OTHERS. INSTEAD, USE HUMOR TO UPLIFT AND CONNECT, ENSURING IT ALIGNS WITH YOUR BELIEFS AND STRENGTHENS RELATIONSHIPS RATHER THAN UNDERMINING THEM.

12

The Comfortable Drift

Readers working through this study alongside
The Screwtape Letters may wish to revisit Chapter 12

Chapter 12 Major Takeaways

In Chapter Twelve, Screwtape discusses the gradual process by which a soul can be led away from God without dramatic or obvious sins. He describes how small, seemingly insignificant compromises and distractions can slowly dull the Patient's spiritual sensitivity and lead him further away from God. Screwtape emphasizes the effectiveness of subtlety in temptation—encouraging Wormwood to keep the Patient comfortable and complacent, avoiding any dramatic temptations that might awaken him to his spiritual state. The goal is to make the Patient drift gradually, so he doesn't realize the danger until it's too late. Screwtape notes that this slow, almost imperceptible decline is more effective than a sudden fall.

Discussion Questions

1. Why does Screwtape emphasize the effectiveness of subtle, gradual temptation over dramatic sins?

"For this reason we must pay much closer attention to what we have heard, lest we drift away."
Hebrews 2:1

2. What are some examples of "small" sins or distractions that might lead someone to drift away from God?

> *"Be of sober spirit, be watchful. Your adversary the devil prowls around like a roaring lion, seeking someone to devour."*
> *1 Peter 5:8*

3. How does Screwtape suggest that comfort and complacency can be used to weaken the Patient's faith?

> *"Guard your heart with all diligence, For from it flow the springs of life."Proverbs 4:23*

4. What does Screwtape mean when he says, "Indeed the safest road to Hell is the gradual one"?

> *"And let us not lose heart in doing good, for in due time we will reap if we do not grow weary."*
> *Galatians 6:9*

5. How can we stay vigilant in our spiritual lives to avoid the gradual drift that Screwtape describes?

"But each one is tempted when he is carried away and enticed by his own lust. [15] Then when lust has conceived, it gives birth to sin, and when sin is fully matured, it brings forth death."
James 1:14-15

6. In what ways can regular self-examination help prevent the subtle spiritual decline Screwtape advocates for?

"Search me, O God, and know my heart; Try me and know my anxious thoughts; And see if there be any hurtful way in me, And lead me in the everlasting way."
Psalm 139:23–24

REAL WORLD APPLICATIONS

GUARD AGAINST THE GRADUAL DRIFT AWAY FROM YOUR FAITH BY REGULARLY ASSESSING YOUR SPIRITUAL PRACTICES AND PRIORITIES. SMALL COMPROMISES CAN LEAD TO SIGNIFICANT DISTANCE FROM GOD OVER TIME, SO STAY VIGILANT IN MAINTAINING YOUR COMMITMENT TO PRAYER, COMMUNITY, AND SPIRITUAL GROWTH. THIS PROACTIVE APPROACH HELPS YOU REMAIN STRONG IN YOUR FAITH AND RESISTANT TO SUBTLE TEMPTATIONS.

13 🖋

The Power of a Real Moment

Readers working through this study alongside
The Screwtape Letters may wish to revisit Chapter 13

Chapter 13 Major Takeaways

In Chapter Thirteen, Screwtape is frustrated because the Patient has experienced a positive spiritual turn. The Patient has repented and felt a renewed sense of God's presence, partly triggered by enjoying simple pleasures, like a walk in the countryside and reading a good book, which reconnected him with his authentic self and God. Screwtape criticizes Wormwood for allowing the Patient to experience such pleasures, as they reminded him of the deeper, truer aspects of life that align with God's will. Screwtape warns that when the Patient enjoys real pleasures, it draws him closer to God and away from the superficial temptations that Wormwood has been using. He advises that the best approach now is to encourage the Patient to become prideful about his recent spiritual progress, thereby undermining it.

Discussion Questions

1. Why does Screwtape consider the Patient's enjoyment of simple pleasures a setback for their plans?

"But He gives greater grace. Therefore it says, 'God is opposed to the proud, but gives grace to the humble.'"
James 4:6

2. How can real, innocent pleasures draw someone closer to God?

"Instruct those who are rich in this present age not to be haughty or to set their hope on the uncertainty of riches, but on God, who richly supplies us with all things to enjoy."
1 Timothy 6:17

3. What dangers does Screwtape see in the Patient becoming aware of his spiritual progress?

"Delight yourself in Yahweh; And He will give you the requests of your heart."
Psalm 37:4

4. How can the enjoyment of life's simple pleasures be a form of worship or a way to connect with God?

"Set your mind on the things above, not on the things that are on earth."
Colossians 3:2

5. What strategies can we use to avoid falling into pride after making spiritual progress?

"Finally, brothers, whatever is true, whatever is dignified, whatever is right, whatever is pure, whatever is lovely, whatever is commendable, if there is any excellence and if anything worthy of praise, consider these things."
Philippians 4:8

6. How can we ensure that our spiritual growth is sustained and not undermined by subtle temptations like pride?

"Thus says Yahweh, 'Let not a wise man boast in his wisdom, and let not the mighty man boast in his might, let not a rich man boast in his riches; but let him who boasts boast in this, that he understands and knows Me.'"
Jeremiah 9:23–24

REAL WORLD APPLICATIONS

EMBRACE AND APPRECIATE THE SIMPLE JOYS IN LIFE, SUCH AS NATURE OR MEANINGFUL CONVERSATIONS, AS THEY CAN RECONNECT YOU WITH GOD AND BRING GENUINE CONTENTMENT. THESE MOMENTS OF TRUE PLEASURE CAN STRENGTHEN YOUR SPIRITUAL LIFE, REMINDING YOU OF GOD'S PRESENCE IN EVERYDAY EXPERIENCES AND HELPING YOU RESIST THE LURE OF SUPERFICIAL OR HARMFUL TEMPTATIONS.

14 ✒

The Weight of Humility

Readers working through this study alongside
The Screwtape Letters may wish to revisit Chapter 14

Chapter 14 Major Takeaways

In Chapter Fourteen, Screwtape is concerned because the Patient has developed genuine humility, which is a serious threat to their plans. Screwtape explains that true humility involves a realistic view of oneself, where the Patient can acknowledge his strengths and weaknesses without pride or false modesty. Screwtape warns Wormwood to avoid letting the Patient enjoy this newfound humility, as it could lead to even greater spiritual strength. Instead, Screwtape suggests that Wormwood should try to corrupt the Patient's humility by making him aware of it, thereby turning it into pride. Alternatively, Wormwood could push the Patient toward false humility, where he downplays his abilities or refuses to acknowledge them, which can also be a form of pride. The goal is to shift the Patient's focus from God back to himself.

Discussion Questions

1. What is true humility according to Screwtape, and why is it a threat to their plans?

"Do nothing from selfish ambition or vain glory, but with humility of mind regard one another as more important than yourselves."
Philippians 2:3

2. How does Screwtape suggest Wormwood can turn the Patient's humility into a new form of pride?

"Humble yourselves in the presence of the Lord, and He will exalt you."
James 4:10

3. What is the difference between true humility and false humility, and how can false humility be dangerous?

"He has told you, O man, what is good; And what does Yahweh require of you But to do justice, to love lovingkindness, And to walk humbly with your God?"
Micah 6:8

4. How can becoming aware of one's humility lead to pride, according to Screwtape?

"And whoever exalts himself shall be humbled, and whoever humbles himself shall be exalted."
Matthew 23:12

5. What practices can help us cultivate genuine humility without falling into the traps Screwtape describes?

"For through the grace given to me I say to everyone among you not to think more highly of himself than he ought to think; but to think so as to have sound thinking, as God has allotted to each a measure of faith."
Romans 12:3

6. Why is focusing on God rather than oneself essential for true humility?

"Let another praise you, and not your own mouth; A stranger, and not your own lips."
Proverbs 27:2

REAL WORLD APPLICATIONS

PRACTICE TRUE HUMILITY BY ACKNOWLEDGING YOUR STRENGTHS AND WEAKNESSES WITHOUT FALLING INTO PRIDE OR FALSE MODESTY. FOCUS ON SERVING OTHERS AND GIVING CREDIT TO GOD FOR YOUR ABILITIES. BY KEEPING YOUR PERSPECTIVE BALANCED AND CENTERED ON GOD, YOU CAN AVOID THE PITFALLS OF SELF-CENTEREDNESS AND FOSTER GENUINE SPIRITUAL GROWTH.

15

Time As a Trap

Readers working through this study alongside
The Screwtape Letters may wish to revisit Chapter 15

Chapter 15 Major Takeaways

In Chapter Fifteen, Screwtape discusses the importance of time and how humans should be kept focused on either the past or the future, but never the present. He explains that the future is the most useful to them because it is uncertain and filled with anxiety, which can be exploited. The present, on the other hand, is where time touches eternity, making it the most spiritually beneficial state for the Patient. Screwtape emphasizes that focusing on the future leads to fear, worry, and ultimately a detachment from God, while living in the present fosters faith, obedience, and trust.

Discussion Questions

1. Why does Screwtape prefer the Patient to focus on the future rather than the present?

"So do not worry about tomorrow, for tomorrow will worry about itself. Each day has enough trouble of its own."
Matthew 6:34

2. How can an obsession with the future negatively impact one's faith and relationship with God?

"Be anxious for nothing, but in everything by prayer and petition with thanksgiving let your requests be made known to God."
Philippians 4:6

3. What does Screwtape mean when he says the present is where time touches eternity?

"Yet you do not know what your life will be like tomorrow. You are just a vapor that appears for a little while and then vanishes away."
James 4:14

4. How can living in the present strengthen one's faith?

"This is the day which Yahweh has made; Let us rejoice and be glad in it."
Psalm 118:24

5. What practical steps can we take to focus more on the present and less on the future?

"For He says, 'At the acceptable time I listened to you, and on the day of salvation I helped you.' Behold, now is 'the acceptable time,' behold, now is 'the day of salvation.'"
2 Corinthians 6:2

6. How can focusing on the present moment help us better align our actions with God's will?

"In the morning, Yahweh, You will hear my voice; In the morning I will order my prayer to You and eagerly watch."
Psalm 5:3

REAL WORLD APPLICATIONS

FOCUS ON LIVING IN THE PRESENT MOMENT RATHER THAN WORRYING EXCESSIVELY ABOUT THE FUTURE. TRUST THAT GOD IS IN CONTROL AND USE TODAY TO GROW SPIRITUALLY AND SERVE OTHERS. BY STAYING PRESENT AND GROUNDED IN YOUR FAITH, YOU CAN REDUCE ANXIETY AND BETTER ALIGN YOUR ACTIONS WITH GOD'S WILL, LEADING TO A MORE PEACEFUL AND FULFILLING LIFE.

16 🪶

Pews and Pretenses

*Readers working through this study alongside
The Screwtape Letters may wish to revisit Chapter 16*

Chapter 16 Major Takeaways

In Chapter Sixteen, Screwtape discusses the Patient's churchgoing habits, aiming to exploit them to weaken his faith. Screwtape suggests either pushing the Patient towards church-hopping, where he never settles in one place, or encouraging him to focus on superficial aspects of worship. By keeping the Patient critical of sermons and church members, Screwtape hopes to foster a sense of superiority and dissatisfaction, leading him away from genuine worship and community. The goal is to make the Patient's church experience more about personal preference and critique than about spiritual growth and connection with God.

Discussion Questions

1. How does Screwtape suggest using the Patient's churchgoing habits to weaken his faith?

"Not forsaking our own assembling together, as is the habit of some, but encouraging one another, and all the more as you see the day drawing near."
Hebrews 10:25

2. Why might church-hopping be spiritually detrimental according to Screwtape?

> *"Now I exhort you, brothers, by the name of our Lord Jesus Christ, that you all agree and that there be no divisions among you, but that you be made complete in the same mind and in the same judgment."*
> *1 Corinthians 1:10*

3. How can a critical attitude towards church services and members affect one's faith?

> *"Doing nothing from selfish ambition or vain glory, but with humility of mind regarding one another as more important than yourselves."*
> *Philippians 2:3*

4. What is the danger of making church more about personal preference than spiritual growth?

> *"Be of the same mind toward one another; do not be haughty in mind, but associate with the humble. Do not be wise in your own mind."*
> *Romans 12:16*

5. How can we cultivate a healthy attitude towards church attendance and worship?

> *"With all humility and gentleness, with patience, bearing with one another in love, being diligent to keep the unity of the Spirit in the bond of peace."*
> *Ephesians 4:2-3*

6. What are the benefits of committing to a single church community despite its imperfections?

> *"Let all bitterness and anger and wrath and shouting and slander be put away from you, along with all malice. Instead, be kind to one another, tender-hearted, graciously forgiving each other, just as God in Christ also has graciously forgiven you."*
> *Ephesians 4:31–32*

REAL WORLD APPLICATIONS

APPROACH YOUR CHURCH INVOLVEMENT WITH HUMILITY AND AN OPEN HEART, AVOIDING THE TEMPTATION TO JUDGE OTHERS OR VIEW YOURSELF AS SPIRITUALLY SUPERIOR. FOCUS ON WORSHIPING GOD AND BUILDING GENUINE CONNECTIONS WITHIN YOUR COMMUNITY. THIS ATTITUDE FOSTERS UNITY, DEEPENS YOUR FAITH, AND HELPS YOU GROW SPIRITUALLY WITHOUT FALLING INTO THE TRAP OF PRIDE OR DIVISION.

17

Virtue With a Vice Aftertaste

Readers working through this study alongside
The Screwtape Letters may wish to revisit Chapter 17

Chapter 17 Major Takeaways

In Chapter Seventeen, Screwtape focuses on the sin of gluttony, but not in the way most people think of it. Instead of the typical overindulgence in food, Screwtape discusses "The Gluttony of Delicacy," where a person becomes excessively picky or demanding about their food, insisting on having things "just so." This form of gluttony is subtle and socially acceptable, making it an effective tool for leading the Patient into selfishness and away from love and consideration for others. By focusing on his own preferences and desires, the Patient becomes more self-centered and less able to see the needs or feelings of those around him.

Discussion Questions

1. How does Screwtape redefine gluttony in this chapter, and why is it effective in leading people away from God?

"Doing nothing from selfish ambition or vain glory, but with humility of mind regarding one another as more important than yourselves, not merely looking out for your own personal interests, but also for the interests of others."
Philippians 2:3-4

2. Why might "The Gluttony of Delicacy" be more dangerous than traditional overindulgence?

"Whether, then, you eat or drink or whatever you do, do all to the glory of God."
1 Corinthians 10:31

3. How can being overly concerned with personal preferences impact relationships with others?

"When you sit down to dine with a ruler, Understand well what is before you, And you shall put a knife to your throat If you are a man of appetite. Do not desire his delicacies, For it is bread of falsehood."
Proverbs 23:1-3

4. What are the spiritual dangers of becoming overly focused on minor details and preferences in life?

"For the kingdom of God is not eating and drinking, but righteousness and peace and joy in the Holy Spirit."
Romans 14:17

5. How can we identify and avoid the subtle forms of gluttony in our own lives?

"Do not worry then, saying, 'What will we eat?' or 'What will we drink?' or 'What will we wear for clothing?' But seek first His kingdom and His righteousness, and all these things will be added to you."
Matthew 6:31-33

6. What role does humility play in counteracting the "Gluttony of Delicacy"?

"Let each of us please his neighbor for his good, to his building up. For even Christ did not please Himself, but as it is written, 'The reproaches of those who reproached You fell on Me.'"
Romans 15:2–3

REAL WORLD APPLICATIONS

BE AWARE OF HOW EVEN SUBTLE FORMS OF SELFISHNESS, LIKE BEING OVERLY PARTICULAR ABOUT YOUR PREFERENCES, CAN LEAD TO SELF-CENTEREDNESS. PRACTICE GRATITUDE AND FLEXIBILITY, FOCUSING ON THE NEEDS OF OTHERS RATHER THAN INSISTING ON HAVING THINGS YOUR WAY. THIS SHIFT IN MINDSET HELPS CULTIVATE HUMILITY AND STRENGTHENS YOUR RELATIONSHIPS, ALIGNING YOUR ACTIONS MORE CLOSELY WITH THE SELFLESS LOVE THAT GOD CALLS US TO.

18 ✒

Love, Lust, and The Lie

Readers working through this study alongside
The Screwtape Letters may wish to revisit Chapter 18

Chapter 18 Major Takeaways

In Chapter Eighteen, Screwtape discusses the topic of love, particularly romantic love, and how it can be manipulated to lead the Patient away from God. Screwtape explains that humans often confuse different forms of love, such as lust and genuine affection, and that this confusion can be exploited. He describes how the "romantic" idea of being in love can be idolized, leading people to justify selfish or harmful behavior. Screwtape also emphasizes that the Enemy (God) values selfless, sacrificial love, which is a threat to their cause. Wormwood is encouraged to twist the Patient's understanding of love into something self-serving, leading him away from the true, self-giving love that God desires.

Discussion Questions

1. How does Screwtape suggest twisting the Patient's understanding of love to lead him away from God?

"Love is patient, love is kind, is not jealous, does not brag, is not puffed up; it does not act unbecomingly, does not seek its own, is not provoked, does not take into account a wrong suffered; it does not rejoice in unrighteousness, but rejoices with the truth; it bears all things, believes all things, hopes all things, endures all things."
1 Corinthians 13:4-7

2. What are the dangers of confusing different types of love, such as romantic love and lust?

"Husbands, love your wives, just as Christ also loved the church and gave Himself up for her."
Ephesians 5:25

3. Why does Screwtape consider selfless, sacrificial love a threat to their cause?

"The one who does not love does not know God, because God is love."
1 John 4:8

4. How can the idolization of romantic love lead to selfishness or harmful behavior?

"Let love be without hypocrisy—by abhorring what is evil, clinging to what is good."
Romans 12:9

5. What practical steps can we take to cultivate a healthy, God-centered understanding of love?

"Greater love has no one than this, that one lay down his life for his friends."
John 15:13

6. How can we differentiate between true, self-giving love and love that is primarily self-serving?

"Little children, let us not love with word or with tongue, but in deed and truth."
1 John 3:18

REAL WORLD APPLICATIONS

RECOGNIZE THE DIFFERENCE BETWEEN GENUINE LOVE AND SELFISH DESIRE. IN YOUR RELATIONSHIPS, STRIVE TO LOVE SELFLESSLY, PRIORITIZING THE WELL-BEING AND GROWTH OF OTHERS RATHER THAN SEEKING PERSONAL GRATIFICATION. BY ALIGNING YOUR UNDERSTANDING OF LOVE WITH GOD'S EXAMPLE, YOU CAN BUILD HEALTHIER, MORE FULFILLING RELATIONSHIPS THAT REFLECT TRUE, CHRIST-LIKE LOVE

19 ✐

The Idol Called Love

Readers working through this study alongside
The Screwtape Letters may wish to revisit Chapter 19

Chapter 19 Major Takeaways

In Chapter Nineteen, Screwtape addresses the concept of love, continuing from the previous chapter, but with a focus on God's love for humanity. Screwtape expresses confusion and frustration over the idea that God truly loves human beings. He finds it difficult to understand how an all-powerful being could genuinely care for such flawed creatures. Screwtape considers the possibility that God's love might be a strategy or a form of manipulation, but ultimately, he admits that the concept of selfless love is beyond his comprehension. He instructs Wormwood to use this incomprehensibility to foster doubt in the Patient, leading him to question the reality of God's love.

Discussion Questions

1. Why does Screwtape struggle to understand God's love for humanity?

"For God so loved the world, that He gave His only Son, so that everyone who believes in Him will not perish, but have eternal life."
John 3:16

2. How does Screwtape suggest using the incomprehensibility of God's love to foster doubt in the Patient?

"But God demonstrates His own love toward us, in that while we were yet sinners, Christ died for us."
Romans 5:8

3. What does Screwtape's confusion about love reveal about the nature of evil?

"In this is love, not that we loved God, but that He loved us and sent His Son to be the propitiation for our sins."
1 John 4:10

4. Why might it be important for believers to understand and accept God's love, even when it seems beyond comprehension?

"But God, being rich in mercy, because of His great love with which He loved us, even when we were dead in our transgressions, made us alive together with Christ—by grace you have been saved—"
Ephesians 2:4-5

5. How can the concept of selfless love, as seen in God's actions, challenge and transform our understanding of relationships?

"Give thanks to Yahweh, for He is good, For His lovingkindness endures forever."
Psalm 136:26

6. What practical steps can we take to remind ourselves of God's love when we face doubts?

"But I trust in Your lovingkindness; My heart shall rejoice in Your salvation. I will sing to Yahweh, because He has dealt bountifully with me."
Psalm 13:5–6

REAL WORLD APPLICATIONS

TRUST IN GOD'S LOVE, EVEN WHEN IT SEEMS BEYOND UNDERSTANDING. INSTEAD OF DOUBTING WHETHER YOU ARE WORTHY OF HIS LOVE, EMBRACE IT FULLY AND ALLOW IT TO TRANSFORM YOUR LIFE. BY ACCEPTING GOD'S UNCONDITIONAL LOVE, YOU CAN OVERCOME FEELINGS OF UNWORTHINESS AND GROW IN CONFIDENCE, KNOWING THAT YOUR VALUE COMES FROM BEING LOVED BY HIM.

20

The Cult of Superficial Beauty

Readers working through this study alongside
The Screwtape Letters may wish to revisit Chapter 20

Chapter 20 Major Takeaways

In Chapter Twenty, Screwtape advises Wormwood on how to exploit the Patient's sexual desires to lead him away from God. Screwtape discusses the Enemy's (God's) design for human sexuality, which is meant to strengthen the bond between a man and a woman within marriage. However, Screwtape suggests that Wormwood should twist these desires, leading the Patient towards lust and the pursuit of shallow, self-gratifying relationships. He also mentions the idea of "sexual taste" being manipulated by societal trends, making people desire what is unnatural or harmful. By distorting the Patient's understanding of love and sexuality, Screwtape hopes to drive a wedge between him and God.

Discussion Questions

1. How does Screwtape suggest using the Patient's sexual desires to lead him away from God?

"Flee sexual immorality. Every other sin that a man commits is outside the body, but the sexually immoral man sins against his own body. Or do you not know that your body is a sanctuary of the Holy Spirit who is in you, whom you have from God, and that you are not

your own? For you were bought with a price: therefore glorify God in your body."
1 Corinthians 6:18-20

2. What is the Enemy's (God's) design for human sexuality, according to Screwtape?

"Marriage is to be held in honor among all, and the marriage bed is to be undefiled, for the sexually immoral and adulterers God will judge."
Hebrews 13:4

3. How can societal trends influence and distort one's understanding of sexuality?

"But I say to you that everyone who looks at a woman to lust for her has already committed adultery with her in his heart."
Matthew 5:28

4. Why is it important to understand the difference between love and lust in the context of relationships?

"But sexual immorality and all impurity or greed must not even be named among you, as is proper among saints."
Ephesians 5:3

5. How can believers guard against the temptation to view sexuality in a way that is contrary to God's design?

"For this is the will of God, your sanctification—that you abstain from sexual immorality; that each of you know how to possess his own vessel in sanctification and honor, not in lustful passion, like the Gentiles who do not know God."
1 Thessalonians 4:3-5

6. What role does gratitude play in maintaining a healthy perspective on love and relationships?

"How can a young man keep his way pure? By keeping it according to Your word."
Psalm 119:9

REAL WORLD APPLICATIONS

GUARD YOUR HEART AND MIND AGAINST LETTING LUST OR DISTORTED DESIRES TAKE OVER YOUR RELATIONSHIPS. FOCUS ON CULTIVATING LOVE THAT IS ROOTED IN RESPECT, COMMITMENT, AND SELFLESSNESS, AS INTENDED BY GOD. BY KEEPING YOUR RELATIONSHIPS PURE AND HONORING GOD'S DESIGN FOR LOVE, YOU CREATE STRONGER, MORE MEANINGFUL CONNECTIONS THAT UPLIFT AND SUPPORT YOUR SPIRITUAL JOURNEY.

21

The Myth of 'My Time'

Readers working through this study alongside
The Screwtape Letters may wish to revisit Chapter 21

Chapter 21 Major Takeaways

In Chapter Twenty-One, Screwtape focuses on the concept of ownership, particularly the Patient's sense of ownership over his time, possessions, and even his life. Screwtape explains that encouraging the Patient to believe that he "owns" his time, his body, and his life is an effective way to foster frustration, impatience, and anger when his expectations are not met. Screwtape points out that when the Patient's perceived rights are violated—whether it's his time being interrupted or his plans being thwarted—he becomes more susceptible to temptation. Screwtape's goal is to keep the Patient focused on what he believes is "his" and to feel constantly wronged when life doesn't go as he expects.

Discussion Questions

1. How does Screwtape suggest using the Patient's sense of ownership to lead him into frustration and anger?

"The earth is Yahweh's, as well as its fullness, The world, and those who dwell in it."
Psalm 24:1

2. Why is the concept of ownership a powerful tool in leading someone away from spiritual growth?

"Come now, you who say, 'Today or tomorrow we will go to such and such a city, and spend a year there and engage in business and make a profit.' Yet you do not know what your life will be like tomorrow. You are just a vapor that appears for a little while and then vanishes away. Instead, you ought to say, 'If the Lord wills, we will live and also do this or that.'"
James 4:13-15

3. What does Screwtape say about the Patient's belief that he owns his time?

"Or do you not know that your body is a sanctuary of the Holy Spirit who is in you, whom you have from God, and that you are not your own? For you were bought with a price: therefore glorify God in your body."
1 Corinthians 6:19-20

4. How can a Christian's understanding of stewardship help counteract the temptation to view time, possessions, and life as personal property?

"Then He said to them, 'Beware, and be on your guard against every form of greed, for not even when one has an abundance does his life consist of his possessions.'"
Luke 12:15

5. What are the dangers of feeling entitled to control over our lives, according to Screwtape?

"The heart of man plans his way, But Yahweh directs his steps."
Proverbs 16:9

6. How can we practice surrendering our sense of ownership to God in our daily lives?

"Commit your works to Yahweh And your plans will be established."
Proverbs 16:3

REAL WORLD APPLICATIONS

RELEASE THE ILLUSION OF OWNERSHIP OVER YOUR TIME, POSSESSIONS, AND LIFE. RECOGNIZE THAT EVERYTHING YOU HAVE IS A GIFT FROM GOD, AND PRACTICE STEWARDSHIP BY USING THESE RESOURCES ACCORDING TO HIS WILL. BY LETTING GO OF ENTITLEMENT AND EMBRACING GRATITUDE, YOU CAN REDUCE FRUSTRATION AND FOSTER A DEEPER SENSE OF PEACE AND PURPOSE IN YOUR DAILY LIFE.

22 ✒

Pleasure's Double Agent

Chapter 22 Major Takeaways

In Chapter Twenty-Two, Screwtape is deeply frustrated because the Patient has fallen in love with a Christian woman who embodies strong virtues. Screwtape despises her for her genuine faith, humility, and purity, and he fears the positive influence she will have on the Patient. Screwtape instructs Wormwood to exploit the sexual aspect of the relationship, encouraging lust to distort their love. He also suggests that Wormwood should try to sow discord by encouraging the Patient to idolize the woman or become overly possessive, which could lead to jealousy or other negative emotions. Screwtape ends the letter with a personal outburst of anger towards Wormwood, revealing the strain the situation is putting on him.

Discussion Questions

1. Why is Screwtape so frustrated with the Patient's relationship with the Christian woman?

"Do not be unequally yoked with unbelievers. For what partnership have righteousness and lawlessness, or what fellowship has light with darkness?"
2 Corinthians 6:14

2. How does Screwtape suggest exploiting the sexual aspect of the Patient's relationship to lead him astray?

"Husbands, love your wives, just as Christ also loved the church and gave Himself up for her, so that He might sanctify her, having cleansed her by the washing of water with the word,"
Ephesians 5:25-26

3. What potential dangers does Screwtape identify in the Patient idolizing or becoming possessive of the woman?

"An excellent wife, who can find? For her worth is far above pearls."
Proverbs 31:10

4. Why does Screwtape view the woman's virtues as a threat to their cause?

"Love is patient, love is kind, it is not jealous; love does not brag, it is not puffed up; it does not act unbecomingly, it does not seek its own, it is not provoked, it does not take into account a wrong suffered; it does not rejoice in unrighteousness, but rejoices with the truth; it bears all things, believes all things, hopes all things, endures all things."1 Corinthians 13:4-7

5. How can the Patient's love for this woman strengthen his faith rather than lead him into temptation?

> "Let marriage be held in honor among all, and the marriage bed be undefiled, for fornicators and adulterers God will judge." Hebrews 13:4

6. What can believers learn from this chapter about the importance of choosing a partner who shares and strengthens their faith?

> "Little children, guard yourselves from idols."
> 1 John 5:21

REAL WORLD APPLICATIONS

BE CAUTIOUS OF IDOLIZING YOUR RELATIONSHIPS, EVEN WITH FELLOW BELIEVERS. FOCUS ON LOVING OTHERS WHILE KEEPING GOD AT THE CENTER OF YOUR LIFE. BY MAINTAINING THIS BALANCE, YOU CAN AVOID TURNING RELATIONSHIPS INTO SOURCES OF PRIDE OR POSSESSIVENESS, ENSURING THAT YOUR CONNECTIONS WITH OTHERS STRENGTHEN RATHER THAN DISTRACT FROM YOUR SPIRITUAL JOURNEY.

23

Faith Without Foundation

Readers working through this study alongside
The Screwtape Letters may wish to revisit Chapter 23

Chapter 23 Major Takeaways

In Chapter Twenty-Three, Screwtape advises Wormwood to exploit the Patient's interest in Christianity, especially its social and political aspects. Screwtape encourages Wormwood to shift the Patient's focus from the core of his faith—his relationship with God—to secondary issues like political causes or social justice. By making the Patient believe that his faith is primarily about advancing a particular agenda rather than following Christ, Wormwood can lead him into self-righteousness and division. Screwtape wants the Patient to think of Christianity as a means to an end, rather than an end in itself, thus distorting the true purpose of faith.

Discussion Questions

1. How does Screwtape suggest shifting the Patient's focus from his relationship with God to secondary issues?

"But seek first His kingdom and His righteousness, and all these
things will be added to you."
Matthew 6:33

2. Why does Screwtape see danger in the Patient understanding Christianity as an end in itself rather than a means to an end?

"But more than that, I count all things to be loss because of the surpassing value of knowing Christ Jesus my Lord, for whom I have suffered the loss of all things, and count them but rubbish so that I may gain Christ."
Philippians 3:8

3. What are the risks of intertwining faith with political or social agendas, according to Screwtape?

"Set your mind on the things above, not on the things that are on earth."
Colossians 3:2

4. How can focusing on secondary issues create division within the Church?

"First of all, then, I exhort that petitions and prayers, requests and thanksgivings, be made for all men, for kings and all who are in authority, so that we may lead a tranquil and quiet life in all godliness and dignity."
1 Timothy 2:1-2

5. What strategies can believers use to keep their faith centered on Christ rather than on secondary issues?

> *"For the kingdom of God is not eating and drinking, but righteousness and peace and joy in the Holy Spirit."*
> *Romans 14:17*

6. Why is it important for Christians to distinguish between the core of their faith and secondary matters?

> *"Let us also lay aside every weight and the sin which so easily entangles us, and let us run with endurance the race that is set before us, fixing our eyes on Jesus, the author and perfecter of faith."*
> *Hebrews 12:1–2*

REAL WORLD APPLICATIONS

KEEP YOUR FAITH CENTERED ON YOUR RELATIONSHIP WITH GOD RATHER THAN ALLOWING IT TO BECOME SOLELY ABOUT SOCIAL OR POLITICAL CAUSES. WHILE THESE CAUSES CAN BE IMPORTANT, THEY SHOULD NOT OVERSHADOW YOUR PRIMARY FOCUS ON FOLLOWING CHRIST. BY PRIORITIZING YOUR SPIRITUAL GROWTH, YOU CAN ENGAGE WITH THE WORLD IN A WAY THAT REFLECTS GOD'S LOVE AND TRUTH WITHOUT BECOMING DISTRACTED OR DIVIDED BY SECONDARY ISSUES.

24

Pride In the Pew

Readers working through this study alongside
The Screwtape Letters may wish to revisit Chapter 24

Chapter 24 Major Takeaways

In Chapter Twenty-Four, Screwtape discusses the dangers of the Patient becoming spiritually proud due to his relationship with his new Christian friends and his girlfriend. Screwtape advises Wormwood to encourage the Patient to feel superior to others who are not part of his new "inner circle." By fostering a sense of exclusivity and elitism, Screwtape hopes to draw the Patient into spiritual pride, making him more focused on his status within the group than on his relationship with God. This pride can lead to a judgmental attitude, division, and a false sense of righteousness, which ultimately distances the Patient from true humility and spiritual growth.

Discussion Questions

1. How does Screwtape suggest using the Patient's new Christian friends to foster spiritual pride?

"But He gives greater grace. Therefore it says, 'God is opposed to the proud, but gives grace to the humble.'"
James 4:6:

2. Why is spiritual pride particularly dangerous to the Patient's faith?

"Do nothing from selfish ambition or vain glory, but with humility of mind regard one another as more important than yourselves."
Philippians 2:3

3. What are the risks of viewing one's faith as a status symbol rather than a relationship with God?

"For through the grace given to me I say to everyone among you not to think more highly of himself than he ought to think, but to think so as to have sound thinking, as God has allotted to each a measure of faith."
Romans 12:3

4. How can a sense of exclusivity within a Christian group lead to division and a lack of genuine fellowship?

"You younger men, likewise, be subject to your elders; and all of you, clothe yourselves with humility toward one another, for 'God is opposed to the proud, but gives grace to the humble.'"
1 Peter 5:5

5. What practical steps can the Patient take to avoid falling into the trap of spiritual pride?

"And whoever exalts himself shall be humbled, and whoever humbles himself shall be exalted."
Matthew 23:12

6. How does true humility differ from the false humility that Screwtape might encourage?

"Let another praise you, and not your own mouth; A stranger, and not your own lips."
Proverbs 27:2

REAL WORLD APPLICATIONS

BE WARY OF SPIRITUAL PRIDE, ESPECIALLY WHEN YOU FEEL PART OF AN "ELITE" GROUP WITHIN YOUR FAITH COMMUNITY. REMAIN HUMBLE AND FOCUSED ON GOD'S GRACE RATHER THAN COMPARING YOURSELF TO OTHERS. BY PRACTICING HUMILITY, YOU CAN MAINTAIN GENUINE CONNECTIONS WITH OTHERS AND AVOID THE DIVISIVENESS THAT COMES FROM FEELING SUPERIOR IN YOUR SPIRITUAL JOURNEY.

25 🖋

Addicted To the New

Readers working through this study alongside
The Screwtape Letters may wish to revisit Chapter 25

Chapter 25 Major Takeaways

In Chapter Twenty-Five, Screwtape explores the concept of "the horror of the Same Old Thing," a human tendency to become bored with routine and seek out novelty. Screwtape explains that this desire for constant change can be exploited by leading the Patient to become restless and dissatisfied with the familiar aspects of his faith, relationships, and life in general. Screwtape suggests that by encouraging the Patient to chase after novelty, whether in religion, relationships, or entertainment, Wormwood can prevent him from developing true contentment and spiritual depth. The pursuit of the new and exciting can distract the Patient from the deeper, lasting satisfaction found in God and steady spiritual practices.

Discussion Questions

1. How does Screwtape suggest using the human desire for novelty to lead the Patient away from God?

"Jesus Christ is the same yesterday and today and forever."
Hebrews 13:8

2. What are the dangers of becoming dissatisfied with the familiar aspects of faith or life?

"But godliness is a means of great gain when accompanied by contentment. For we have brought nothing into the world, so we cannot take anything out of it either."
1 Timothy 6:6-7

3. How can the pursuit of novelty in religion lead to spiritual shallowness?

"Not that I speak from want, for I learned to be content in whatever circumstances I am. I know how to get along with humble means, and I also know how to live in abundance. In any and all things I have learned the secret of being filled and going hungry, both of having abundance and suffering need."
Philippians 4:11-12

4. Why does Screwtape believe that the constant desire for change can be a powerful tool for temptation?

"The fear of Yahweh leads to life, So that one may sleep satisfied, not visited by evil."
Proverbs 19:23

5. What practical steps can the Patient take to cultivate contentment and resist the temptation to constantly seek novelty?

"Yet those who wait for Yahweh Will gain new strength; They will mount up with wings like eagles, They will run and not get tired, They will walk and not become weary."
Isaiah 40:31

6. How does the concept of "the horror of the Same Old Thing" relate to modern culture's emphasis on constant change and innovation?

"Oh how I love Your law! It is my meditation all the day."
Psalm 119:97

REAL WORLD APPLICATIONS

RESIST THE TEMPTATION TO CONSTANTLY SEEK NOVELTY OR CHANGE IN YOUR SPIRITUAL LIFE. INSTEAD, FIND VALUE IN THE CONSISTENCY OF ROUTINE PRACTICES LIKE PRAYER, WORSHIP, AND FELLOWSHIP. BY APPRECIATING THE DEPTH THAT COMES WITH STEADFASTNESS, YOU CAN GROW SPIRITUALLY WITHOUT BEING DISTRACTED BY THE PURSUIT OF NEW EXPERIENCES THAT MAY LEAD TO SUPERFICIALITY.

26 ✒

The Romance of Control

*Readers working through this study alongside
The Screwtape Letters may wish to revisit Chapter 26*

Chapter 26 Major Takeaways

In Chapter Twenty-Six, Screwtape discusses the dangers of unselfishness and how it can be manipulated to create tension and resentment in relationships. He explains that both men and women have different notions of what it means to be unselfish, often leading to misunderstandings and conflicts. Screwtape advises Wormwood to exploit these differences by encouraging the Patient to focus on his own idea of unselfishness while resenting what he perceives as selfishness in others. By doing this, the Patient can be led into self-righteousness, bitterness, and division in his relationships, all while believing he is being virtuous.

Discussion Questions

1. How does Screwtape suggest manipulating the concept of unselfishness to create tension in relationships?

"Doing nothing from selfish ambition or vain glory, but with humility of mind regarding one another as more important than yourselves; not merely looking out for your own personal interests, but also for the interests of others."
Philippians 2:3-4

2. What are the differences between how men and women might perceive unselfishness, according to Screwtape?

"Love is patient, love is kind, it is not jealous; love does not brag, it is not puffed up; it does not act unbecomingly, it does not seek its own, is not provoked, does not take into account a wrong suffered."
1 Corinthians 13:4-5

3. Why is self-righteousness a danger when practicing unselfishness?

"Be devoted to one another in brotherly love; giving preference to one another in honor."
Romans 12:10

4. How can misunderstanding or misapplying unselfishness lead to bitterness in relationships?

"For you were called to freedom, brothers. Only do not turn your freedom into an opportunity for the flesh, but through love serve one another."
Galatians 5:13

5. What is the difference between true unselfishness and the distorted version that Screwtape encourages?

"A new commandment I give to you, that you love one another, even as I have loved you, that you also love one another. By this all will know that you are My disciples, if you have love for one another."
John 13:34-35

6. How can believers practice true unselfishness in a way that strengthens relationships?

"Every way of a man is right in his own eyes, But Yahweh weighs the hearts."
Proverbs 21:2

REAL WORLD APPLICATIONS

PRACTICE TRUE UNSELFISHNESS BY FOCUSING ON THE NEEDS AND WELL-BEING OF OTHERS WITHOUT EXPECTING ANYTHING IN RETURN. AVOID THE TRAP OF PERFORMING "UNSELFISH" ACTS OUT OF OBLIGATION OR FOR RECOGNITION, AS THIS CAN LEAD TO RESENTMENT. GENUINE SELFLESSNESS, ROOTED IN LOVE, STRENGTHENS RELATIONSHIPS AND REFLECTS THE HUMILITY AND GRACE THAT GOD DESIRES IN OUR INTERACTIONS WITH OTHERS.

27 ✒

Faith Without Questions

Readers working through this study alongside
The Screwtape Letters may wish to revisit Chapter 27

Chapter 27 Major Takeaways

In Chapter Twenty-Seven, Screwtape discusses the role of prayer in the Patient's life. He advises Wormwood to distort the Patient's prayers, encouraging him to pray for outcomes rather than aligning his will with God's. Screwtape suggests that if the Patient can be made to pray for specific, material results, rather than focusing on spiritual growth or God's will, his prayers will be less effective and more self-centered. Screwtape also proposes encouraging the Patient to pray in vague, abstract terms or to focus on his feelings during prayer rather than on God. By doing so, Wormwood can lead the Patient to frustration when his prayers seem unanswered or to develop a superficial prayer life.

Discussion Questions

1. How does Screwtape suggest distorting the Patient's prayers to make them less effective?

> *"Pray, then, in this way: 'Our Father who is in heaven, Hallowed be Your name. Your kingdom come. Your will be done, On earth as it is in heaven.'"*
> *Matthew 6:9-10*

2. Why is it problematic for the Patient to focus on specific outcomes in his prayers?

"Be anxious for nothing, but in everything by prayer and petition with thanksgiving let your requests be made known to God."
Philippians 4:6

3. What does Screwtape mean by encouraging the Patient to pray in vague, abstract terms?

"And this is the confidence which we have before Him, that, if we ask anything according to His will, He hears us."
1 John 5:14

4. How can focusing on feelings during prayer lead to a superficial prayer life?

"You ask and do not receive, because you ask with wrong motives, so that you may spend it on your pleasures."
James 4:3

5. What is the significance of aligning one's prayers with God's will rather than personal desires?

"And in the same way the Spirit also helps our weakness; for we do not know how to pray as we should, but the Spirit Himself intercedes with groanings too deep for words."
Romans 8:26

6. How can believers cultivate a more meaningful and effective prayer life?

"But as for me, I trust in You, O Yahweh; I say, 'You are my God.' My times are in Your hand; Deliver me from the hand of my enemies and from those who pursue me."
Psalm 31:14–15

REAL WORLD APPLICATIONS

FOCUS YOUR PRAYERS ON SEEKING ALIGNMENT WITH GOD'S WILL RATHER THAN MERELY ASKING FOR SPECIFIC OUTCOMES. AVOID MAKING PRAYER ABOUT YOUR FEELINGS OR DESIRES, AND INSTEAD, CULTIVATE A DEEPER CONNECTION WITH GOD BY TRUSTING HIS WISDOM. THIS APPROACH LEADS TO A MORE MEANINGFUL AND EFFECTIVE PRAYER LIFE, WHERE YOUR FAITH IS STRENGTHENED BY A TRUE RELATIONSHIP WITH GOD RATHER THAN THE PURSUIT OF PERSONAL GAIN.

28 ✒

The Padded Path to Hell

*Readers working through this study alongside
The Screwtape Letters may wish to revisit Chapter 28*

Chapter 28 Major Takeaways

In Chapter Twenty-Eight, Screwtape reflects on the inevitability of death and how Wormwood should approach it concerning the Patient. Screwtape acknowledges that death is something the devils can't fully control and that it's better for them if a person dies in a state of spiritual weakness rather than strength. He discusses the potential dangers if the Patient lives a long life, as it might allow him time to grow spiritually and strengthen his relationship with God. However, Screwtape also notes that long life can lead to complacency, making the Patient more vulnerable to temptation. Ultimately, Screwtape advises Wormwood to keep the Patient focused on fears and anxieties about the future, to keep him from living fully in the present and growing spiritually.

Discussion Questions

1. Why does Screwtape express concern about the Patient living a long life?

"For to me, to live is Christ and to die is gain."
Philippians 1:21

2. How does Screwtape suggest using the Patient's fear of death to his advantage?

"I have fought the good fight, I have finished the course, I have kept the faith; in the future there is laid up for me the crown of righteousness, which the Lord, the righteous Judge, will award to me on that day—and not only to me, but also to all who have loved His appearing."
2 Timothy 4:7-8

3. What are the potential dangers of spiritual complacency as one ages, according to Screwtape?

"Even though I walk through the valley of the shadow of death, I fear no evil, for You are with me; Your rod and Your staff, they comfort me."
Psalm 23:4

4. How can the fear of death hinder spiritual growth and a relationship with God?

"And inasmuch as it is appointed for men to die once and after this comes judgment."
Hebrews 9:27

5. What role does trust in God's plan play in overcoming the fear of death?

"Jesus said to her, 'I am the resurrection and the life; he who believes in Me will live even if he dies, and everyone who lives and believes in Me will never die. Do you believe this?'"
John 11:25-26

6. How can believers maintain spiritual vigilance and growth throughout their lives, especially as they age?

"So teach us to number our days, That we may present to You a heart of wisdom."
Psalm 90:12

REAL WORLD APPLICATIONS

IN TIMES OF PHYSICAL OR EMOTIONAL EXHAUSTION, RELY ON GOD'S STRENGTH RATHER THAN YOUR OWN. RECOGNIZE THAT CHALLENGES AND WEARINESS ARE OPPORTUNITIES TO DEEPEN YOUR TRUST IN GOD'S PROVISION AND CARE. BY TURNING TO HIM IN YOUR WEAKEST MOMENTS, YOU BUILD RESILIENCE AND MAINTAIN YOUR SPIRITUAL INTEGRITY, ENSURING THAT FATIGUE DOESN'T LEAD TO SPIRITUAL COMPROMISE.

29 🖋

The Coward's Crown

Readers working through this study alongside
The Screwtape Letters may wish to revisit Chapter 29

Chapter 29 Major Takeaways

In Chapter Twenty-Nine, Screwtape discusses the fear and hatred that arise during wartime, as the Patient is living through a war. Screwtape suggests that Wormwood should exploit these emotions to lead the Patient away from God. He advises that the Patient be encouraged to hate not just the enemy nation, but also individuals within it, thereby turning his emotions into personal, consuming hatred. Screwtape explains that fear and hatred can be powerful tools, as they can cloud the Patient's judgment, lead him to commit sins he might otherwise avoid, and ultimately separate him from God. Screwtape emphasizes that while fear may push the Patient closer to God out of desperation, hatred will pull him further away.

Discussion Questions

1. How does Screwtape suggest using the emotions of fear and hatred during wartime to lead the Patient away from God?

"There is no fear in love, but perfect love casts out fear, because fear involves punishment, and the one who fears has not been perfected in love."
1 John 4:18

2. Why does Screwtape believe that hatred is more effective than fear in leading the Patient away from God?

"But I say to you, love your enemies and pray for those who persecute you."
Matthew 5:44

3. What are the spiritual dangers of allowing fear to dominate one's thoughts and actions?

"Never taking your own revenge, beloved— instead leave room for the wrath of God, for it is written, 'Vengeance is Mine, I will repay,' says the Lord."
Romans 12:19

4. How can hatred, even when justified by external circumstances like war, erode one's spiritual life?

"Be anxious for nothing, but in everything by prayer and petition with thanksgiving let your requests be made known to God. And the peace of God, which surpasses all comprehension, will guard your hearts and your minds in Christ Jesus."
Philippians 4:6-7

5. What strategies can believers use to resist the temptation to give in to fear and hatred, especially during difficult times like war?

"Hatred stirs up strife, But love covers all transgressions."
Proverbs 10:12

6. How does focusing on God's love and forgiveness help combat the negative effects of fear and hatred?

"Do not be overcome by evil, but overcome evil with good."
Romans 12:21

REAL WORLD APPLICATIONS

RESIST THE PULL OF FEAR AND HATRED, ESPECIALLY IN CHALLENGING TIMES LIKE CONFLICT OR CRISIS. INSTEAD, FOCUS ON LOVE, FORGIVENESS, AND TRUST IN GOD'S SOVEREIGNTY. BY CHOOSING TO RESPOND WITH COMPASSION AND FAITH, YOU CAN PREVENT NEGATIVE EMOTIONS FROM OVERWHELMING YOU AND MAINTAIN YOUR SPIRITUAL HEALTH, EVEN IN THE MOST DIFFICULT CIRCUMSTANCES.

30

Blows That Build

Readers working through this study alongside
The Screwtape Letters may wish to revisit Chapter 30

Chapter 30 Major Takeaways

In Chapter Thirty, Screwtape discusses the increasing pressure on the Patient as the war intensifies. The Patient is now experiencing the physical and emotional strains of being in a dangerous situation, which Screwtape hopes Wormwood can use to his advantage. Screwtape advises Wormwood to amplify the Patient's fatigue, fear, and anger, driving him to despair and making him more susceptible to temptation. Screwtape also suggests exploiting the Patient's exhaustion to weaken his resistance to sinful thoughts and actions, hoping that the Patient will become spiritually drained and easier to manipulate. Despite the challenges, Screwtape warns Wormwood not to let the Patient turn to God in his distress, as this could lead to spiritual renewal and growth.

Discussion Questions

1. How does Screwtape suggest using the Patient's physical and emotional exhaustion to lead him into temptation?

"Yet those who hope in Yahweh Will gain new power; They will mount up with wings like eagles, They will run and not get tired, They will walk and not become weary."
Isaiah 40:31

2. What role does fear play in weakening the Patient's spiritual defenses during times of crisis?

> *"Come to Me, all who are weary and heavy-laden, and I will give you rest."*
> *Matthew 11:28*

3. Why is despair considered a particularly dangerous state for the Patient, according to Screwtape?

> *"God is our refuge and strength, A very present help in trouble."*
> *Psalm 46:1*

4. How can physical fatigue impact the Patient's ability to resist temptation and maintain his spiritual practices?

> *"And He has said to me, 'My grace is sufficient for you, for power is perfected in weakness.' Most gladly, therefore, I will rather boast in my weaknesses, so that the power of Christ may dwell in me."*
> *2 Corinthians 12:9*

5. What strategies can believers use to stay spiritually strong during times of physical and emotional exhaustion?

"Consider it all joy, my brothers, when you encounter various trials, knowing that the testing of your faith brings about perseverance. And let perseverance have its perfect work, so that you may be perfect and complete, lacking in nothing."
James 1:2-4

6. Why does Screwtape warn Wormwood about the potential for the Patient to turn to God in his distress?

"For You have been my help; And in the shadow of Your wings I sing for joy. My soul clings to You; Your right hand upholds me."
Psalm 63:7–8

REAL WORLD APPLICATIONS

DURING TIMES OF INTENSE PRESSURE OR FEAR, GUARD AGAINST LETTING EXHAUSTION LEAD YOU INTO DESPAIR OR TEMPTATION. SEEK GOD'S STRENGTH TO SUSTAIN YOU AND CONTINUE YOUR SPIRITUAL PRACTICES EVEN WHEN YOU'RE WEARY. BY TRUSTING IN GOD'S PRESENCE AND RELYING ON HIS POWER, YOU CAN NAVIGATE CHALLENGES WITH RESILIENCE AND MAINTAIN YOUR FAITH, AVOIDING THE PITFALLS THAT COME WITH SPIRITUAL FATIGUE.

31 ✒

Heaven's Triumph Hell's Defeat

*Readers working through this study alongside
The Screwtape Letters may wish to revisit Chapter 31*

Chapter 31 Major Takeaways

In Chapter Thirty-One, Screwtape writes to Wormwood after the Patient's death. Despite Wormwood's efforts, the Patient has died in a state of grace, having remained faithful to God. Screwtape is furious and disappointed, as the Patient has now escaped their clutches and entered eternity with God. Screwtape describes the Patient's experience as he realizes the true nature of God and heaven, which is beyond what he could have imagined. Screwtape's letter reveals his own despair and hatred for God, acknowledging that Wormwood has failed in his mission. The chapter closes with Screwtape threatening to consume Wormwood as punishment for his failure.

Discussion Questions

1. How does Screwtape react to the Patient's death and his entrance into heaven?

"I have fought the good fight, I have finished the course, I have kept the faith; in the future there is laid up for me the crown of righteousness, which the Lord, the righteous Judge, will award to me on that day—and not only to me, but also to all who have loved His

appearing."
2 Timothy 4:7-8

2. What is significant about the Patient's final moments and his experience of death?

"For I am convinced that neither death, nor life, nor angels, nor rulers, nor things present, nor things to come, nor powers, nor height, nor depth, nor any other created thing, will be able to separate us from the love of God, which is in Christ Jesus our Lord."
Romans 8:38-39

3. Why is Screwtape so enraged at Wormwood's failure, and what does this reveal about the nature of evil in the story?

"In My Father's house are many dwelling places; if it were not so, I would have told you, for I go to prepare a place for you. And if I go and prepare a place for you, I will come again and receive you to Myself, that where I am, there you may be also."
John 14:2-3

4. What does the Patient's victory over temptation and his faithfulness to God demonstrate about the power of faith?

"And He will wipe away every tear from their eyes; and there will no longer be any death; there will no longer be any mourning, or crying, or pain; the first things passed away."
Revelation 21:4

5. How does the Patient's realization of the true nature of God and heaven contrast with the world's view of death?

"Surely goodness and lovingkindness will pursue me all the days of my life, And I will dwell in the house of Yahweh forever."
Psalm 23:6

6. What lesson can believers draw from the conclusion of the Patient's story?

"Yahweh will guard your going out and your coming in From now until forever."
Psalm 121:8

REAL WORLD APPLICATIONS

TRUST IN GOD'S ULTIMATE VICTORY, KNOWING THAT FAITHFULNESS LEADS TO ETERNAL LIFE WITH HIM. EVEN WHEN FACING LIFE'S FINAL MOMENTS OR GREATEST CHALLENGES, KEEP YOUR FOCUS ON GOD'S LOVE AND GRACE. BY HOLDING FAST TO YOUR FAITH UNTIL THE END, YOU CAN BE ASSURED OF GOD'S PROMISE OF ETERNAL PEACE AND JOY IN HIS PRESENCE, OVERCOMING ANY FEAR OR DOUBT.

32 ✒

Bonus Chapter

Screwtape and the Age of Distraction

In this creative reflection inspired by *The Screwtape Letters*, Screwtape reflects on the modern era of social media and its potential for temptation, distraction, and spiritual erosion. How might the strategies of hell evolve to exploit today's digital world?

Disclaimer: This bonus chapter is not part of C.S. Lewis's original The Screwtape Letters but is written in the same satirical style to explore how Screwtape's strategies might adapt to modern challenges, such as social media and digital distractions. This addition is meant to encourage thoughtful discussion and is not an official part of Lewis's work.

My Dear Wormwood,

I note with great satisfaction that your Patient has recently embraced that most potent tool of our modern age: social media. Ah, the wonders of this new technology! You must recognize the infinite possibilities it provides for distraction, envy, and the slow erosion of true relationships.

The Enemy, of course, intended these networks to serve as tools for connection, for sharing moments of joy, for bringing His creatures closer together. How laughable! What He fails to realize—though I suspect He knows but allows it anyway—is how effortlessly we can twist these platforms to our advantage.

The first and most obvious advantage is distraction. Encourage your Patient to check his accounts frequently—no, constantly. Each notification, each "like," and each new post offers a momentary thrill, a little spike of pleasure. But more importantly, each one pulls him further away from the present moment, where the Enemy is most likely to speak to him. Keep his attention flitting from one trivial update to the next, and you will soon find that he has little time for the Enemy's whispers of truth, or even for those around him.

Now, on to envy. Social media is a veritable breeding ground for it! Encourage your Patient to compare his life with the carefully curated lives of others. Let him feel the sting of inadequacy as he sees others boasting of their achievements, their relationships, their adventures. You see, Wormwood, they do not post their struggles, their failures, their loneliness. They present a life of perfection, an illusion, and your Patient must believe it to be real. This will lead him to feel that his own life is lacking, that he is somehow less blessed, less fortunate than his peers. And from there, envy will take root, and with it, discontent, self-pity, and a gradual turning away from gratitude to the Enemy.

Furthermore, there is the delicious opportunity to foster vanity and pride. Your Patient will soon begin to curate his own online persona, carefully selecting what to share and what to hide. He will become preoccupied with how others perceive him, seeking validation in the form of "likes" and comments. Over time, his self-worth will become entangled with the number of followers he has, the reactions to his posts, and the approval of strangers. This is fertile ground for pride, Wormwood. Convince him that his value is found in these fleeting affirmations rather than in the Enemy's unchanging love.

Do not overlook the potential for division. Social media, when handled correctly, can deepen existing fissures in society, turning minor disagreements into full-blown conflicts. Encourage your Patient to engage in debates, to share controversial opinions, and to seek out echo chambers that reinforce his views while vilifying others. The more time he spends quarreling online, the less he will spend in genuine conversation, understanding, and reconciliation. The Enemy desires unity, but we thrive on division. Use this tool well, Wormwood.

Lastly, beware of the moments when your Patient begins to recognize the emptiness of this constant engagement. There will be times when he feels the weight of his addiction, when the hollowness of endless scrolling becomes apparent. He may even consider stepping away, seeking silence, or—horror of horrors— turning to the Enemy for comfort. You must be vigilant in these moments. Convince him that these platforms are necessary, that without them, he would be isolated, invisible, unimportant. Reinforce the idea that his online presence is essential to his identity.

In all, Wormwood, remember that technology is neither good nor evil in itself. It is merely a tool, one that we can wield with great efficiency. Social media, when used properly, can be a subtle but powerful means of leading your Patient away from the Enemy's light, step by step, click by click.

Your affectionate uncle,
Screwtape

Glossary of words used in *The Screwtape Letters*

Abjection – A state of extreme humiliation, degradation, or submission.

Apatheia – A state of being free from emotional disturbance; often associated with calmness or indifference.

Ardour – Intense passion or enthusiasm, often in the context of faith or devotion.

Asceticism – A lifestyle characterized by self-discipline and abstention from indulgence, often for religious or spiritual reasons.

Bellicose – Having an aggressive or warlike nature; inclined to fight.

Bureaucracy – A system of government or management that is overly complex, rigid, and inefficient, often used metaphorically to describe Hell's administrative style in the book.

Complacency – A self-satisfied state of mind that leads to a lack of awareness or vigilance, making one vulnerable to spiritual decline.

Coterie – A small, exclusive group of people with shared interests or values.

Cynicism – A distrustful or skeptical attitude, especially toward human motives or religious beliefs.

Debauchery – Excessive indulgence in sensual pleasures, often leading to moral corruption.

Dilettante – A person who dabbles in an art or field of knowledge without serious commitment.

Disillusionment – The feeling of disappointment when realizing that something is not as good as one once believed, often used to weaken faith.

Efficacy – The ability to produce a desired or intended result; effectiveness.

Expedient – A means of achieving an end, especially one that is convenient but possibly improper or immoral.

Felicity – Great happiness or the ability to find appropriate expression for one's thoughts.

Foment – To stir up or incite unrest, conflict, or division.

Furtive – Secretive, sly, or attempting to avoid notice, often describing the way evil operates.

Gluttony of Delicacy – A concept introduced in the book describing an obsession with food preferences and minor comforts rather than sheer excess.

Gusto – Great enthusiasm or enjoyment, often used when describing how humans indulge in pleasures.

Imperturbable – Unable to be disturbed or agitated; calm and collected.

Indulgence – Excessive or unrestrained enjoyment of pleasures, sometimes leading to sin.

Inveterate – Deeply ingrained or long-established, often referring to habits or attitudes that are difficult to change.

Jargon – Specialized language used by a particular group, often difficult for outsiders to understand.

Juncture – A critical point in time, often where a significant decision is made.

Languid – Lacking energy, enthusiasm, or interest, often used to describe spiritual laziness.

Lascivious – Showing an excessive or inappropriate interest in sexual matters.

Maladroit – Clumsy or lacking skill in handling situations.

Mitigated – Made less severe, serious, or painful.

Obfuscate – To deliberately make something unclear or confusing, a tactic often used to lead people astray.

Obsequious – Excessively submissive or eager to please, often in a self-serving way.

Peevish – Easily irritated or annoyed.

Perfunctory – Carried out with minimal effort or care, often used to describe empty religious practices.

Perturb – To disturb, unsettle, or make anxious.

Philological – Relating to the study of language, especially historical and literary aspects.

Pragmatism – A practical approach to problems, focusing on results rather than theories or principles.

Querulous – Complaining in a whining or petulant manner.

Repine – To feel discontent or to complain, often about one's circumstances.

Respite – A short period of relief or rest from something difficult or unpleasant.

Sardonic – Mocking or cynical, often in a sharp or scornful way.

Scruples – Moral or ethical considerations that restrain one from making certain choices.

Solicitude – Care or concern for someone or something.

Sophistry – Clever but misleading reasoning, often used to deceive.

Stoicism – The philosophy of enduring pain or hardship without showing emotion, which can sometimes be misapplied in a spiritual sense.

Supine – Lying face upward or figuratively showing a passive, weak, or lazy attitude.

Temporality – The state of being temporary or worldly, as opposed to eternal or spiritual.

Timorous – Showing fear or hesitation; lacking confidence.

Trough – A low or declining point in one's spiritual or emotional state, often following a period of enthusiasm or growth.

Triviality – Something of little importance, often used by Screwtape to keep humans distracted from deeper spiritual truths.

Vainglory – Excessive pride or boastfulness, especially in achievements or appearance.

Wiles – Cunning strategies or tricks meant to deceive or manipulate.

Winsome – Attractive or charming in an innocent or engaging way.

www.ingramcontent.com/pod-product-compliance
Lightning Source LLC
Chambersburg PA
CBHW051324120626
46547CB00015B/2376